EXPLORING WORLD CULTURES

Kenya

Alicia Z. Klepeis

Cavendish
Square

New York

Published in 2018 by Cavendish Square Publishing, LLC
243 5th Avenue, Suite 136, New York, NY 10016

CPSIA Compliance Information: Batch #CS17CSQ

All websites were available and accurate when this book was sent to press.

Library of Congress Cataloging-in-Publication Data

Names: Klepeis, Alicia, 1971- author.
Title: Kenya / Alicia Z. Klepeis.
Other titles: Exploring world cultures.
Description: New York : Cavendish Square Publishing, 2018. |
Series: Exploring world cultures
Identifiers: LCCN 2016046366 (print) | LCCN 2016046742 (ebook) |
ISBN 9781502625045 (pbk.) | ISBN 9781502625052 (6 pack) | ISBN 9781502625328
(library bound) | ISBN 9781502625069 (E-book)
Subjects: LCSH: Kenya--Juvenile literature. | Kenya--Civilization.
Classification: LCC DT433.522 .K54 2017 (print) | LCC DT433.522 (ebook) |
DDC 967.62--dc23
LC record available at https://lccn.loc.gov/2016046366

Editorial Director: David McNamara
Editor: Kristen Susienka
Copy Editor: Rebecca Rohan
Associate Art Director: Amy Greenan
Designer: Joseph Macri
Production Coordinator: Karol Szymczuk
Photo Research: J8 Media

Printed in the United States of America

Contents

Introduction

Kenya is a country in Africa. It has lots of special celebrations and traditions. Early humans began living in Kenya millions of years ago. Different people have ruled what is now Kenya during its history. Today, it is a free country. Kenya's government is a **democracy**.

People in Kenya have many kinds of jobs. Many people grow food or raise animals on farms. Others work in factories, hotels, or schools.

Kenya has lots of beautiful places to visit. It has mountains, grasslands, beaches, and deserts. People come from all over the world to see Kenya's wildlife. The country is home to more than fifty national parks and **reserves**. People also visit Nairobi and Mombasa, its two largest cities.

Kenyans enjoy music, storytelling, and many other arts. People in Kenya like eating different kinds of food. They also enjoy playing sports. Kenya is an exciting country to explore.

A beautiful sunrise on Diani Beach in Kenya

Kenya is located in East Africa. It is about twice the size of the state of Nevada and covers 224,081 square miles (580,367 square kilometers).

This map shows Kenya's major roads, cities, lakes, and rivers.

Kenya borders Ethiopia, Somalia, South Sudan, Tanzania, and Uganda. The Indian Ocean is to the east. Lake Victoria is to the west.

Kenya has different landscapes. Near the Indian Ocean is a low, grassy area. The ground rises as you go inland. Kenya has flat areas called plateaus and mountains in its center.

Kenya's Animals and Plants

Kenya is home to giraffes, rhinoceroses, and more. Unique trees, like the baobab and acacia, grow here.

West of Nairobi (Kenya's capital), the landscape slopes down to the Great Rift Valley. This is a huge tear in Earth's crust. Volcanoes and lakes are in this area.

Kenya lies just north of the equator. Temperatures are hot all year round. Along the coast, it is warmer and wetter than farther inland.

Kenya's Lake Turkana has jade green water. The color comes from blue-green algae.

Scientists think that Kenya may have been home to the earliest humans. People (and their early ancestors) have lived in what is now Kenya for millions of years.

This photo shows the defensive wall of Fort Jesus, built in 1593.

At least 1,400 years ago, **Arabs** started settling near Kenya's coasts. They built trading places here. This led to contact with people from India, Persia, and other Arab areas.

In 1498, the Portuguese explorer Vasco da Gama arrived in Kenya. Portuguese settlers tried to take over Kenya's coastal areas. They were unsuccessful.

The British took over Kenya in 1895. In 1920, Kenya became a British colony. In 1963, Kenya gained independence from Britain. Since then, some leaders have not run the country fairly. Today, Kenyans are working toward a better future.

Jomo Kenyatta

Jomo Kenyatta was Kenya's first president. He ruled from 1964 to 1978.

A photo of Jomo Kenyatta around 1960

Government

Kenya is a democracy. The country is divided into forty-seven counties. Kenya's capital is Nairobi.

The Kenyan government has three parts:

1) Legislative: This part of the

Kenya's National Parliament Building in Nairobi.

government is known as Parliament. People in Parliament write new laws.

2) Judicial: The courts make up this part of Kenya's government. They follow the nation's constitution. The latest constitution took effect in 2010. It describes all of Kenya's basic laws.

FACT!

Kenyan citizens can vote when they are eighteen years old.

3) Executive: The president, deputy president, and the **cabinet** ministers make up this part of the government. The president runs the government. The president is also the head of state.

Kenya's parliament is made up of two houses. The Senate has 67 members. The National Assembly has 349 members. Parliament meets in Nairobi to pass laws.

Women in Parliament

Eighty-six women are serving in Kenya's eleventh parliament. This is the highest number ever to serve in Kenyan history.

The Economy

Kenya has one of the larger economies in Africa. It is an important transportation and trading area in East Africa. Kenya trades with countries around the world. The country's money is called a shilling.

Flowers from Kenya are sent all over the world.

About 80 percent of Kenyan workers are involved with agriculture. They may grow crops or raise animals like cows or goats. Kenyan farmers grow corn, wheat, sugarcane, and fruit. The country also produces dairy products, fish, poultry, and beef.

Some Kenyans work in hospitals, schools, and banks. Tourism is an important industry here. Over one million tourists visit Kenya each year. Other workers have jobs in museums, stores, and hotels.

Factories in Kenya make lots of different products. Examples include clothing, furniture, cement, and plastic items.

Flower Power

Kenya is one of the world's largest exporters of cut flowers. Its roses and carnations are popular in Europe, Russia, and the United States.

Kenya's people, plants, and animals need clean air and clean water to live. Some parts of Kenya do not have these things. Nairobi is one of the world's most polluted cities. Why? There are lots of cars

In Nairobi, traffic jams create more pollution in the air.

in Nairobi. The gas they burn makes the air dirty. Some people burn plastics to get rid of trash. This is not healthy.

Many Kenyans do not have clean water. Some water gets dirty from chemicals used on farms. In other places, trash and human waste pollutes the water. Recycling is getting more popular in Kenya. It will help clean up Kenya.

Kenyan Electricity

Kenya gets about 42 percent of its electricity from fossil fuels like coal and gas.

The Masinga hydroelectric plant

In recent years, Kenya has had some terrible droughts. It is hard for people to get the water they need for everyday use.

Many different animals and plants live in Kenya. Some are now threatened. **Poachers** kill some of these animals. Sometimes new buildings take away their homes.

FACT!

There are fewer than six hundred black rhinoceroses left in the wild in Kenya.

More than forty-five million people live in Kenya. It is one of the largest countries in Africa.

Kenya is home to more than forty **ethnic groups**. The Kikuyu people make up about 22 percent

A Maasai woman wears traditional clothing and beadwork.

of Kenyans. Kenya's second-largest group is the Luhya people. They make up about 14 percent of Kenyans. They tend to live in western Kenya. The Luo people are the third-largest group. The Luos, who live in rural areas, often fish in Lake Victoria. Smaller ethnic groups include the Kalenjin, Kisii, and Meru peoples.

Nearly four million people live in Kenya's biggest city, Nairobi.

Kenya's many ethnic groups have their own traditions. No single group in Kenya makes up a majority of the nation's population.

The Maasai People

The Maasai people live in a huge area of southern Kenya and Tanzania. They are traditionally cattle herders and are known for their beadwork.

The people of Kenya live in different ways. About 75 percent of Kenyans live in rural areas. People here often make a living by farming. Some grow crops or raise animals to sell. Others grow food to feed their families.

These women manage crops in Machakos, Kenya.

Many Kenyans who live near Lake Victoria depend on the lake for food. Sadly, overfishing and pollution threaten the lake's supply of fish.

The unemployment rate in Kenya is quite high, around 40 percent.

About 25 percent of Kenyans live in cities and towns. Life for many Kenyan city dwellers is hard. Nairobi is home to many poor areas. Kibera is the biggest of these areas. The

Schoolchildren raise their hands during a class lesson at school in Nairobi.

government is working hard to improve Kibera. New houses and health clinics are being built.

Women's Roles in Kenya

Traditionally, Kenyan women have worked at home and on farms. More women today work outside of the home. They have jobs as teachers, office and factory workers, and more.

Religion

Religion is an important part of many Kenyans' lives. Kenya has no official religion. All Kenyans are free to believe in what they want.

All Saints Cathedral is in Nairobi.

More than 80 percent of Kenya's people are Christian. More than half of Kenyan Christians are Protestant. There are also large numbers of Catholic people in Kenya. Most Christians in Kenya go to church regularly. All Christians share some beliefs and traditions. They celebrate Easter and Christmas.

Gospel music is popular in Kenya. Many church services involve music and dancing.

About 11 percent of Kenyans are Muslim. They worship in buildings called mosques. Small groups of people follow traditional religions in Kenya. They believe in good and bad spirits, which can influence peoples' lives.

People dance and sing during a church service.

Kenya's Indian Population

Among Kenya's Indian population are people who follow the Hindu and Sikh religions.

21

Language

People in Kenya speak many different languages. The country has two official languages: English and Swahili.

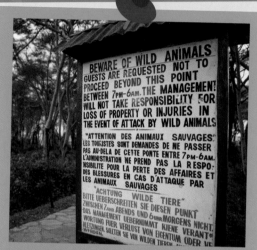

This sign gives warnings to people in English, French, and German.

Kenya's government uses English when writing legal documents. Big businesses (like international ones) also use English. So do universities.

Swahili is a Bantu language. People speak this language in much of East Africa and in South Africa. It is often used in small businesses throughout Kenya.

FACT!

More than one hundred million people around the world speak Swahili.

Students learn both English and Swahili in primary schools. TV and radio programs are often broadcast in both languages, too. Many government documents and newspapers are printed in Swahili and English.

It is quite common for Kenyans to speak at least three languages. One of these is likely to be the language of their ethnic group.

Sheng: An Urban Language

Sheng is a popular language in Kenyan cities. It combines elements of English, Swahili, and other ethnic languages.

People in Kenya celebrate many kinds of art. Music and dance are two of the most important art forms here. Traditionally, different ethnic groups in Kenya have created their own unique music.

Drums of different shapes and sizes are for sale.

People often play music during ceremonies or when dancing.

The Embu people are known for their skill at dancing on stilts.

24

Many instruments play at the same time in Kenyan music. One common instrument is the drum.

Kenya has festivals all year round. Some celebrate religious events. Others focus on tribal rituals. Kenya also has several public holidays. People in Kenya celebrate Independence Day (also called Jamhuri Day) on December 12. This holiday marks the day in 1963 when Kenya became a new independent nation. Kenyans celebrate with parades, feasts, and dancing.

Storytelling: Kenyan Style

Many traditional Kenyan folktales feature animals as main characters. Music may also accompany the storyteller's voice.

Fun and Play

There are many ways to have fun in Kenya. Soccer is the country's most popular sport. Volleyball, basketball, boxing, and rugby are also well liked here. Cricket is a favorite sport, too. Secondary schools in Kenya offer many sporting competitions for girls and boys.

Mancala is one of the oldest games in the world.

People can hike in the country's national parks and reserves. Those who enjoy rock climbing can visit Hell's Gate National Park. Beach lovers have a choice of many options on the Indian Ocean.

26

FACT!

Mount Kenya is 17,057 feet (5,199 meters) tall. It challenges mountain climbers every year.

Mount Kenya

Lots of Kenyans like to play games. *Bao* is a popular board game here. It involves moving seeds or stones around a board.

Many urban Kenyans enjoy going to the movies. People also like watching TV and listening to radio programs.

Track and Field

Kenyans are some of the world's top track and field athletes. Kenyans won thirteen track and field medals at the 2016 Summer Olympics in Brazil.

Food

People in Kenya eat many kinds of food. Some people like eating pineapples, mangoes, and papayas. Green vegetables, potatoes, and sweet potatoes are popular, too.

Many kinds of fruits are on display at a market in Nairobi.

Most Kenyans eat what is in season and available locally. They do not tend to eat frozen or canned foods. Families cook their meals. This is especially true in the rural areas of Kenya.

Ugali is a staple in many Kenyans' diet. It is a thick porridge made from corn flour and water.

Ugali is cheap and nutritious. Kenyans serve it with vegetables or meat.

Beverages in Kenya

Kenyans probably drink tea more than any other beverage.

Near the coast, Kenyans eat more fish. Different ethnic groups have their own preferred foods, too. For example, the Kikuyu tend to eat more lentils, corn, and beans. The Maasai get much of their nutrition by drinking a mixture of cattle blood and milk.

FACT!

Samosas are a popular snack food in Kenya. They are traditionally from India.

Glossary

Arab A member of the Semitic people originally from the Arabian peninsula and neighboring territories.

cabinet A group of advisors who help the leader of a government.

democracy A system of government in which leaders are chosen by the people.

ethnic group Groups of people who share a common culture or ancestry.

poacher A person who hurts animals and takes different animal parts, like an elephant's tusks, to sell.

reserve A large area of land where wild animals can live protected by humans.

Find Out More

Books

Bartell, Jim. *Kenya*. Minnetonka, MN: Bellwether
Media, 2011.

Kalman, Bobbie. *Spotlight on Kenya*. New York:
Crabtree Publishing Company, 2013.

Website

Kenya

http://kids.nationalgeographic.com/explore/

countries/kenya/#kenya-reserve.jpg

Video

Time for School Kenya: Joab

http://www.pbslearningmedia.org/resource/vtl07.

la.rv.text.kenyaclass/a-look-at-a-kenyan-classroom

This video shows the experience of a first grader

named Joab in a crowded Kenyan classroom.

Index

About the Author

Alicia Z. Klepeis began her career at the National Geographic Society. She is the author of many kids' books, including *Trolls*, *The World's Strangest Foods*, *Francisco's Kites*, and *A Time for Change*. She lives with her family in upstate New York.